101 WAYS WITH FLOWERS

Published by BBC Books
BBC Worldwide Ltd, Woodlands,
80 Wood Lane, London W12 0TT

First published for
Marks & Spencer in 2003
This edition published in 2005
Reprinted 2006, 2007
Copyright © BBC Worldwide 2003
Please see page 223 for a list of the
contributors.

ISBN-13: 978 0 563 52259 1
ISBN-10: 0 563 52259 3

Edited by Alison Willmott
Commissioning Editor: Vivien Bowler
Project Editor: Julia Charles
Series Design: Claire Wood
Book Design: Kathryn Gammon
Design Manager: Annette Peppis
Production Controller: Christopher Tinker

Set in Amasis MT and ITC Officina Sans
Printed and bound in Italy by LEGO SpA
Colour origination by Butler & Tanner

BBC Worldwide would like to thank the
following for providing photographs and
permission to reproduce copyright material.
While every effort has been made to trace
and acknowledge all copyright holders, we
would like to apologize should there have
been any errors or omissions.

All photographs © *BBC Good Homes*
magazine 2003 with the following
exceptions: pages 33, 35, 65, 89, 91, 93, 95,
97, 133 and 157 © *BBC Homes & Antiques*
magazine 2003; pages 37, 39, 41, 43, 45, 67,
69, 71, 73, 75, 77, 99, 101, 159, 197, 199,
201, 203, 205, 207 and 209 supplied
courtesy of The Plants and Flowers
Association.

101 WAYS WITH FLOWERS
STYLISH HOME IDEAS

Julie Savill

BBC **Good** **Homes**

CONTENTS

INTRODUCTION

There's no denying that flowers do something quite magical to a room. Add a few blooms to a space that looks lifeless and suddenly the mood lightens, colours look fresh and you can't help but feel more relaxed and at home.

One thing we should all do is stop considering flowers as an infrequent luxury only to be enjoyed on special occasions. It's lovely to be given flowers as a gift but it's even nicer to indulge yourself on a regular basis and if you buy what's in season and plentiful there's no reason why it should be an expensive extravagance. Stores such as Marks & Spencer offer an affordable and convenient way to buy flowers with your weekly shop and even supermarkets have improved the choice and quality of their flowers, so all you need is a few clever ways to display

them to make an instant difference to your home.

101 Ways with Flowers isn't a flower arranging book in the traditional sense but more of a source book of ideas and information to get you thinking about what is possible. Of course, all the ideas here are to be copied but they are also to be adapted and improved upon to suit you and your home. So, if you see an idea you like using carnations but you prefer gerbera, go ahead, swap the flowers and create something new and individual.

Modern flower arranging relies far more on chic, casual displays than on massed formal bunches so a few flowers can be made to go a long, long way. One of *BBC Good Homes* magazine's regular contributors, and someone who deserves special thanks for all her ideas, is the hugely talented Jane Packer who manages to capture the mood of the moment with a simplicity that you just know you can copy for yourself at home. Many of her projects are featured in *101 Ways with Flowers* and they really do prove that with the right inspiration any of us can create stylish flower arrangements in a matter of minutes.

The blissful thing about today's attitude towards flowers is that there are no real rules and no specialist equipment required. With a little lateral thinking almost anything that will hold water – from an old tin can to a teapot – can be pressed into use as a vase. Florist Jane Hughes has a real flair for flowers and unusual ways to use them and deserves our thanks for the witty, creative ideas you'll find in this book.

At *BBC Good Homes* magazine we have worked with some of the very best florists and we would like to thank Nick Green who was the very first florist to contribute to the magazine, Marcus Crane for his beautiful and romantic arrangements and The Plants and Flowers Association for all their ideas and support.

Julie Savill, Editor
BBC Good Homes magazine

Peas plus

Use your imagination and combine flowers with other natural materials to give a simple display an individual look. Vegetables offer an irresistible selection of colours, shapes and textures, and ordinary, everyday ones can look just as effective as the more exotic varieties. This display teams sweet peas with their edible namesakes, the bright green of the peas forming a striking contrast with the delicate pinks and mauves of the petals. Arrange the flowers in a clear glass vase, pack in the peas so that they hide the stems, and then add water.

TIP
Although sweet peas are short-lived as cut flowers, they are easy to grow from seed, so if you have a garden it could provide a constant supply during the summer months.

Shades of green

If brightly coloured blooms are a bit too brash for your taste, an all-green arrangement makes a serene and sophisticated alternative. Foliage or green-tinted flowers with sculptural shapes make an elegant statement against a cool, contemporary backdrop. To add interest, mix different textures and shades of green, combining fresh limes with darker emeralds, as in this display. Standing tall in a clear glass vase, arum lilies, spiky papyrus and glossy Swiss cheese plant leaves strike a powerful pose. The vase tapers towards the neck, holding the tall stems firmly in position.

Fruit cocktail

As well as being a feast for the eyes, this exuberant mix of colourful citrus fruit and gerbera heads is a scent sensation, as it has a refreshing fragrance that's pure summer. Simply fill a shallow glass bowl with water, then slice oranges, lemons and limes in half and float them cut side up. Intersperse the fruits with mini gerbera heads in yellow, pink and red, then add a few sprigs of mint for extra scent. This would make a wonderfully aromatic table centrepiece for a summer meal.

Berry tasty

Floating arrangements in shallow glass bowls are strong candidates for use as table centrepieces, and look particularly delicious when they include some juicy fruits. Soft fruits don't deteriorate very quickly when submerged in water, so should last as long as the flowers. Small berries can be layered on top of one another to create bands of colour, and there are plenty of vibrant varieties to choose from. This eye-catching display places cranberries above gooseberries in a bowl half full of water. Purplish-blue cornflower heads float on top, forming a sumptuous contrast with the rich red of the cranberries.

Hang on in there

Roses, a traditional favourite for so many of us,
look just as good in minimalist modern displays as
in old-fashioned bouquets. In this clever arrangement,
nine glowing orange blooms dangle their straight stems
into the water, suspended above a square tank vase
by a grid of sturdy grasses. Use raffia to tie together
the strands of grasses, then trim the ends neatly so that
they extend past the sides of the vase by at least 2cm.
Cut all the rose stems to the same length, slightly
shorter than the depth of the vase, and settle the
heads in the grid.

High style

Paper whites have a dreamy fragrance that will fill your home with the scent of spring. Make the most of them by gathering a big bunch together and anchoring them among sand and pebbles in a deep glass vase. Take a few flowers in one hand, with the stems parallel and the heads massed together. Keep adding more until you form a ball of flowerheads. Tie the stems with ribbon or twine below the blooms, then cut the stems to the same length. Set them in the vase and surround with white sand and gravel. Top up the vase with water.

TIP
Narcissus stems emit a slime that poisons other flowers, so if you want to use freshly cut blooms in a mixed display, first stand them in deep water containing a drop of bleach for 24 hours.

Heads together

When tulips are cheap and abundant in spring, buy a few bunches of your favourite colours and use them to turn tank vases into bright building blocks. Using blooms of one shade in each vase, snip the stems short so that the heads sit beneath the rim, in a shallow amount of water. Include enough stems so that the flowers support each other and remain upright. Fill a few vases with identical arrangements and place them in an orderly row, or even stack them on top of one another for added impact.

TIP
Tulips are heavy drinkers so remember to top up the vases frequently. Unlike most flowers, they prefer the water to be cool rather than lukewarm.

Sun worshippers

Sunflowers are the ultimate feelgood flower, their big cheerful faces glowing with the warmth of Mediterranean summers. They are readily available as cut flowers, last for weeks and have an ebullient enough character to make their own impact, without requiring clever arranging. This resin vase in citrus yellow emphasizes the colour of the flowers, its tone and texture adding a fresh modern edge to their naive rustic appeal. Arrange them casually, loosely grouping a few stems together, and cut them to length so that the large heavy heads sit on the rim of the vase.

TIP
If a few sunflowers in your bunch have damaged petals, simply pull them off. The seedheads look striking on their own or in a display with other flowers.

Eastern promise

With oriental overtones, this stunning arrangement contrasts exotic pink peony heads with the dark metal of a galvanized planter, balancing the flowers on a grid of pretty coloured bamboo. Fill the planter with water and cut bamboo rods to length so that they extend a couple of centimetres beyond the sides of the planter. Tie the rods together with twine to make a simple grid and place over the planter. Cut some peony heads, leaving enough stem to reach the water, then mass them in the centre of the grid.

TIP
If your local florist doesn't stock coloured bamboo, it's easy to paint some yourself in the colour of your choice.

Foam star

These peonies are arranged in a dark red loose-powder form of Oasis, or florist's foam, which fills a clear glass vase and picks up on the punchy pinks of the blooms. Although today's fuss-free displays mean Oasis is not used as much as it once was, the water-absorbent foam still comes in handy for making stems stay exactly where you want them. Traditionally available only in green or brown, it is a secret that florists used to keep well hidden, but nowadays it's snazzy enough to go on show as it also comes in a range of fabulously bright colours.

TIP
Oasis is the name of the best-known brand of florist's foam and the manufacturer of the brighter colours. Your local florist may stock other brands.

Simply red

Scarlet carnation heads bring a touch of floral fancy
to this tray of twinkling candles, as the frilly silhouettes
of the petals cast their reflections in the still water.
To create this sleek contemporary display, choose
a square Japanese-style tray or dish and team it with
white candles of the same shape. Fill the tray with a
small amount of water, then alternate five candles with
five carnation heads, floating the flowers on the water. If
possible, choose flowers in the same colour as the tray
for maximum impact.

Under water

Many modern flower displays have as much going on inside the vase as outside it, and in this one all the interest occurs beneath the water. Make a tower of colour by submerging hydrangea heads in a tall glass cylinder. Fill the vase with crystal clear water, then take one flowerhead at a time and slowly push it down to the bottom, continuing to add more until the vase is about three-quarters full. Pour off any excess water so that the amount left just covers the topmost flowerhead.

Seeing double

Create two arrangements in one by slotting a smaller glass vase inside a large one. For even greater effect, combine different shapes, such as a globe vase inside a square tank. Fill the larger vase with a few centimetres of water, then place a few long leaves or grass stems inside it and fan them out around the curves. Fill a smaller or narrower vase with water, then place it inside the larger one and use it to contain a simple arrangement of flowers or foliage. The displays shown here feature white geraniums and red Singapore orchids.

NewsLink

MERCHANT NAME
NewsLink
GE128 PASSENGER TERM'L
BLDG HK INTL AIRPORT HK
MID:0005275150002
TID:S194368888   8 MAY 09
                      11:12

SIMPSON/BARRIE L

MERCHANT NO: XXXXXXXXXXXXXXXX 3609 S
CARD TYPE: MASTERCARD XX/XX
CARD TYPE/NUMBER
TRANS: SALE
BATCH NO: 000156 REF:010588
RRN: 91278352S26241
APP CODE: 015292Z

EXPIRY

BOOKS & STATIONERY
DATE/TIME
LOCAL AMT: HKD85.00
REF.NO: RATE: USD/HKD 07.8344516
APP CODE
TXN CUR AMT: USD11.43

I have chosen not to use the MasterCard
Currency conversion process and agree
that I will have recourse against
MasterCard concerning the currency
conversion or its disclosure.

I ACKNOWLEDGE SATISFACTORY RECEIPT OF RELATIVE GOODS / SERVICES.

X CARDHOLDER SIGNATURE

B. J. Simpson

NO REFUND

THE ISSUER OF THE CARD IDENTIFIED ON THIS ITEM IS AUTHORIZED TO PAY TH
AMOUNT SHOWN AS TOTAL UPON PROPER PRESENTATION. I PROMISE TO PAY SUC
TOTAL (TOGETHER WITH ANY OTHER CHARGES DUE THEREON) SUBJECT TO AND IN
ACCORDANCE WITH THE AGREEMENT GOVERNING THE USE OF SUCH CARD.

Arton Specialties Co. Ltd.   Tel: 2723 6986   ST-05-24408

BEA Credit Card Interest Free Instalment Programme Terms and Conditions

東亞銀行信用卡免息分期付款計劃細條款及細則

1. 就申請分期付款服務，東亞銀行信用卡或簽帳卡私人賬戶(不包括公司卡)之持卡人(「持卡人」)獲東亞銀行有限公司(「本行」)於其指定的東亞銀行信用卡賬戶(「指定賬戶」)，扣除以分期付款方式購買應付之金額，以購買於此計劃中特定的商戶(「商戶」)提供的貨品或服務。

2. 就持卡人參加此計劃而言：
   (i)「東亞銀行信用卡持卡人合約」(「持卡人合約」)與本條款及細則一併適用，本條款及細則內如對持卡人合約的條款沒有另作指示，本條款及細則以及持卡人合約中凡適用於持卡人合約者，須解釋爲出本條款及細則加以補充者 持卡人合約；及(ii)如持卡人合約的條款及細則與本條款及細則有任何抵觸，在適用於此計劃的範圍內，須以本條款及細則爲準。

3. 本行擁有一切酌情及自主的批核權並可對無需提供理由下拒絕分期付款申請。

4. 每次分期付款申請可獲得之總額不可超越該持卡人於申請時仍享有的剩餘信用額。如指定賬戶的信用額不足以支付此計劃之總金額，本行有權不接納分期付款申請。然而，持卡人可向本行申請增加信用額以彌補不足。本行保留批准或拒絕該等申請有關之細則及自主的權利。

5. 持卡人之分期付款申請一經獲本行批准，本行便以借貸的方式向持卡人提供相等於購買貨物或服務之價格的借貸。本行有權及確認本行可透過與商戶簽訂的協議把該等款項之全部或部份歸還商戶。持卡人同意以分期付款方式清還並上該信貸之款額不包括商戶之定金。第一期款項每月份還持卡人於批核時之款金額須滿足以上所有在當月款額。除非另行通知，分期付款之期數即爲相等於此批核時的期數。本行將根據以下步驟計算每月之分期付款金額：

   (i)除於(iii)及(iv)，每月之分期付款金額相等於持卡人就此計劃獲提供之信貸總額且本行已批核之分期付款期數等額除；及(ii)每月之分期付款金額會調整最爲及本行有權和決達成此批款後加以任何計算得出的調整；及(iii)倘調整每月之分期付款額或調整至本已批核之分期付款期數所需之總數及每月結單所示，分期付款的信貸總額數，該需要便會隨到第一期的每月分之分期付款金額，並須在第一期分期付款金額按第以一併繳清。

   儘管以上所測，持卡人確認本行有權在使越時自主的酌情權下更改或傷腦以上之原則。

6. 每月之分期付款金額將記入指定賬戶及作月結單上列明。且須由持卡人相連持卡人合約的賬及細則繳付。倘若持卡人及持卡人合約列明的到期繳款且低之最低結單前之數繳付最低金額或月結單總結欠，則持十人合約中的逾期費用及／或財務費用將適用。

7. 持卡人有責任確定指定賬戶有充足之信用額以繳付每月分期償還之金額，否則本行將徵收額外之服務及財務費用。

8. 持卡人同意及確認本行並非此計劃之貨物及服務供應商，故它會就商戶提供此計劃提供之貨物及服務承擔任何法律責任。即使持卡人就此計劃向商戶購買之貨物或服務尚未於賬戶交付，全部或部份損失或失效，持卡人仍有每按指定賬戶每月之分期付款金額還本持卡人就此計劃獲提供之信貸。

9. 倘持卡人就此計劃自商戶購入之貨物或服務導分期即付未獲提供，持卡人應在上述物或服務償付之總數會在交易完成及分期付款申請批核後達續清還時。持卡人須察覺明他清楚與日後繼續償付貨物或服務不獲提供之風險，但是他自行決定購買該貨物或服務前及同意及確認本行在分交後每次有未款期限時可以分期付款方式以償付通所有信貸之權利必予承受任何影響。

10. 特別貝出則外，分期付款計劃不可與其他優惠及折扣同時享用。

11. 持卡人同意及確認儘管持卡人退換或更改所購買之貨物或服務得到商戶退還該物或服務的保證，持卡人就此計劃的參與及此計劃之每期付款金額，分期付款期數及條款不可變更。

12. 本行可在行使絕對自主的酌情權下決定在適格當之情況下對指定賬戶、或持卡人生本行之其他賬戶中扣除任何應付之分期付款之餘額或終止持卡人就此計劃之參與。該等情況包括但不限於下列各點：
   (i)指定賬戶被持卡人或本行取消或在收到由他人發出的任何關通知而被取消；(ii)持卡人未能依期償款；及(iii)持卡人違逆逾期於指定賬戶的持卡人合約中之規定或本條款中之任何規定。

13. 持卡人現確認：
   (i)本行對其品質或承擔任何有關產品或服務之品質、供應、送貨、使用、安裝等及其他事宜之責任。(ii)本行亦不會就商品或服務之質素及知識產權之擁有權件任何表述或保證。(iii)任何於商戶提供之貨物或服務，應盡商戶與商戶解決。

14. 持卡人現同意在可能範圍內承諾彌償本行任何因持卡人違反此計劃之責任的損失、損害、費用及開支，包括但不限於償還本行此計劃服務的成本。

15. 持卡人現同意及確認有關此計劃及商戶可按須審認需之需要交與持卡人就執行此計劃而提供之個人資料。

16. 本行可在維終及自主的酌情下隨時更改此計劃之任何條款，而毋須事前通知持卡人取消此計劃。本行並保留向持卡人即時追討所有此未繳付之數聯分及有關之財務費用之權利。

17. 持卡人同意遵守其他分期推廣優惠文件上列所之條款。

18. 本條款及細則之中文本供參考之用。本條款及細則之中、英文本如有歧異，概以英文版本爲準。

如欲取本條款及細則細之英文本或查詢，請致電東亞銀行信用卡客戶服務熱線：3608 6628
For English version or enquiry, please call BEA Credit Card Customer Services Hotline: 3608 6628

NewsLink (S05)

08 May 2009   11:12:10

Timmy Tang   S0512090508-00639578

===

0563522593   85.0   1
101 WAYS WITH FLOWERS $85.0

SUBTOTAL $85.0
TOTAL $85.0
TENDER MASTER $85.0
CHANGE $0.0

===

Boxing clever

Roses look luxurious but can be expensive, so try experimenting with the cheaper short-stemmed specimens. This fashionable idea packs a crowd of orange blooms into a galvanized metal planter. Soak some florist's foam in water, then fit it into the base of the planter. Trim the stems of about 20 roses to the same length, so that the heads sit just above the lip of the planter. Push the stems into the foam, making sure the heads are level, and fill in the gaps beneath the flowers with bun moss.

TIP
Flowers are likely to last longer in an arrangement where the stems are cut short, as water can reach the heads more easily.

Strawberries and cream

A display that looks good enough to eat would make an eye-catching centrepiece for a table or sideboard. Bold amaryllis heads bring an extravagant flavour to any arrangement. Here they are massed together in the centre of a shaped glass dish to form a lush dome of scarlet, which is encircled by a contrasting border of cream-petalled anemones and shaggy gerbera in a pale shade of peach. A charger plate placed underneath the dish adds a decorative finishing touch, the spotted pattern of its border echoing the circle of smaller blooms.

TIP
If you are using an arrangement as a table centrepiece, make sure it is low enough not to block your guests' view across the table or make conversation difficult.

Budding genius

Related to buttercups, ranunculus have big, beautiful heads packed with papery petals, which look good both at bud stage and once the flowers are fully opened. Available in many colours, from delicate pastels to vivid reds and oranges, they can claim a place in many different styles of arrangement. In this chic contemporary display, the frosted glass of the conical container is complemented by white ranunculus buds, arranged in a circle around a single yellow head. They nestle just beneath the rim of the vase on a bed of moraea, its sprays of tiny yellow and green flowers helping to support the heavy ranunculus heads.

Sing the blues

While clear glass vases create an unobtrusive showcase for the natural beauty of flowers and stems, colourful containers can add an extra dimension to a display. The secret is to make the colour work with the flowers. Here, an understated posy of greenish-white anemones surrounded by a collar of furry stachys leaves gets a bold modern treatment when arranged in a tall blue vase. The blue complements the soft grey leaves of the stachys, and their elegant shapes are echoed by the gentle curves of the container.

TIP
A few other types of grey-leaved foliage you could try include sage, artemisia and santolina.

Slick mix

Texture can be as important an ingredient as colour when you are combining two or more types of flowers or other natural materials. An exciting mix can create an individual display – here spiky asclepias seed pods sit alongside small pompon-like heads of yellow matricaria, topped with frilly-petalled fragrant white hyacinths. The wire bowl adds a further texture, giving the display its modern edge. Arrange the flowers in a glass or plastic bowl and place this inside the basket, or line the basket with polythene and fill it with pre-soaked florist's foam.

Cool chrysanths

Chrysanthemums assume a sophisticated character in a display that sticks to a limited palette of white and green. Its appeal is boosted by a mixture of textures: soft pennisetum grass and spiky nigella seed pods combined with rows of small green-centred chrysanthemums, all crowned by a dramatic shaggy-head spider variety. To create the raised effect, use pre-soaked florist's foam that extends beyond the top of the vase. Alternatively, place a second narrow container inside the vase to hold the central chrysanthemum and leaves, then build up the additional material in layers, arranging it in the space between the inner and outer containers.

Lazy days

Set the scene for an alfresco family lunch in summer
with pots of sunny yellow marigolds plucked straight
from the garden. Old tin cans make excellent informal
containers; here their corrugated metal complements
the rustic grey wood of the table while forming a shiny
contrast with its rough texture. Clean out your old food
tins thoroughly, fill them with water, and then place a
few big, droopy marigold blooms in each one, with their
heads resting just above the rim. Add enough foliage
to fill in the gaps.

Nesting instinct

With velvety purple pansies and eggshells nestling among moss in a wire basket, this unusual display would make a good talking point, perhaps as an Easter table decoration. Carefully break the tops off a few eggshells, making sure that the body of the shell remains intact. Line a wire basket with freshly gathered moss, then nestle the shells on top and fill them with water. Cut a few pansy heads, leaving short stems, and arrange them with the stems inside the eggshells so that the water keeps the flowers fresh.

China collection

White china containers are a feature of traditional country kitchens, so raid your cupboards for pots, jugs and vases and line them up along a shelf or mantelpiece to make a charming grouped display. Fill any pots with compost, then plant them with flowering annuals, and use the other containers to show off fresh spring flowers such as narcissus. Sticking to a limited colour theme of yellow and white for the flowers will help to enhance the plain and simple appeal of the china.

Old and new

Add a hint of country charm to a contemporary
room setting with a display of flowers and foliage in
a traditional container. This tall yellow enamel pitcher
plays host to a casual arrangement of chrysanthemums
and dahlias in refreshing colours, which complement
the room's light modern decor. Pay a visit to a car boot
sale or junk shop and you should find it easy to pick
up 'vases' with character. Make sure that they are clean
and watertight before you use them for flowers, or find
a glass or plastic container (a tumbler is ideal) that fits
inside to hold the blooms.

Tall story

This elegant, tree-like display is a modern classic that works well with any strong-stemmed flowers. Arrange a mixture of agapanthus and nerines in your hand, bringing the flowerheads together to make a ball shape. Tie the stems with string, just beneath the flowers. Pull the stems together to make the trunk of the flower tree and trim them all to the same length, then bind near the base using waterproof tape. Put a pinholder in the bowl and push the bound ends of the stems into it so that they stand upright. Cover the pinholder with cobbles and add water.

TIP
A pinholder is an old-fashioned flower arranging tool comprising a bunch of little metal spikes on a base-plate. See if your mum or gran has one tucked away before going out to buy one.

Rich pickings

Mix flowers and foliage gathered from your garden for a simple country-style display. Make this posy using pink roses, white ranunculus, green alchemilla and other assorted foliage, or see what your beds and borders have to offer. Arrange the material loosely in your hand, building from the centre and alternating flowers and foliage as you work. Keep the display loose, almost scruffy, to add to that countryside feel. Secure the stems with garden string and cut them to match the height of the vase. For further country charm, place a few more blooms in an old milk jug beside the main vase.

TIP
Pick flowers from your garden in the early morning or late evening. Place them in water immediately, or the stems will form an air-lock that prevents them drinking.

Bit of rough

Choose chunky organic vases to set a rustic tone. The rough textures and natural shades of stone or terracotta planters form a fascinating contrast with the pretty colours and delicate petals of hydrangeas and roses. Pack plenty of hydrangea heads tightly into a vase, with the stems cut down and hidden from view, and include a collar of leaves beneath the flowers to strengthen the look. Roses would be expensive to use in the same abundance, so try floating just a head or two in a rustic bowl with a layer of coloured gravel at the bottom.

TIP
Porous stone or clay containers not designed specifically as vases may not be watertight, so place a glass or plastic container inside to hold the arrangement.

Pastel palette

There's nothing like strongly scented flowers for bringing the outside indoors, and fragrant hyacinths will add a whiff of spring to your rooms long before the weather warms up. Often grown indoors from bulbs, they are now also widely available as cut flowers, which last extremely well. They come in a broad selection of colours, including exquisitely muted pastels such as this pale pink. These hyacinths are massed with white parrot tulips in stone-coloured pots to create a light, natural effect. If you can't find pots this colour, try painting plain terracotta ones using sample pots of paint, and finish with matt varnish.

TIP
Buy cut hyacinths in tight green bud with the colour barely showing. The stem will continue to grow in water and the head will triple in size as the flower bells open.

Harvest festival

This display celebrates the warm but mellow hues of autumn, which is when hydrangea blooms deepen in colour to rich reds, purples or lilacs. Here, they are complemented beautifully by rosy apples and red skimmia. Huge hydrangea heads look dramatic as cut flowers and, although they are a little pricey, just one or two go a long way when massed with fruit or foliage. Place a smaller column vase inside a large one and fill the gap in between with crab apples. Fill the inner vase with water, arrange the hydrangeas and skimmia, then add a few apples pushed onto sticks, toffee apple style.

TIP
Hydrangeas are prone to wilting. To help keep them fresh, drape damp cloths over the blooms for a few hours after cutting.

Hi-tech hedgerow

A collection of flowers that you might see in any country hedgerow, such as dill flower and cowslip, is given a modern twist when displayed in a designer-style test tube vase. The test tubes are wired together so that they can be adjusted to form different shapes and curves. Cut the flower stems to different lengths to get a random-looking variation in height, then place two or three stems in each test tube. If you use tall, top-heavy flowers, flex the row of test tubes into a zig-zag shape to make it stable.

Meadow fresh

In this informal bouquet, the bold exuberance of a
pair of sunflowers is softened by a surround of foliage
and grasses. The huge blooms sit low among the other
materials, framed by sprays of golden lime bupleurum
and cream-edged dogwood leaves, while feathery
grasses froth out at the base. The homely style of the
display is enhanced by the rough pottery vase with its
buttermilk glaze. Build up the bouquet in your hand,
starting with the sunflowers, then adding the bupleurum
and dogwood and finally the grasses. Cut the stems to
the same length, and bind with twine before placing
in the vase.

Enchanted forest

A fascinating mixture of textures gives this display its unique charm. Left to themselves, a bunch of green parrot tulips massed together in a purple glass bowl would have asserted a mood of modern sophistication, but a collar of rough tangled roots disturbs their cool to add a touch of drama. Twining around the leaves and stems, the roots create an almost sinister air, their woody texture contrasting with the smooth curves and heavy glass of the vase and the satiny petals of the flowers.

Out of the woods

Oak leaves and twigs give a woodland feel to red and
pink blooms, while a plain white glass vase shows off
the richness of their autumn colours. Flat pink sedum
flowerheads contrast with globe-shaped red dahlias and
papery-petalled hydrangeas. The flowers are arranged
in clusters, with all of one type together, to heighten
the contrast between textures. The oak leaves form
a collar beneath them, and more are interspersed
between the flowers to set off their strong hues. Stark
twigs poke wildly from among the blooms, breaking the
neat rounded shape of the display and reinforcing
the woodland inspiration.

Exotic mood

In this simple but striking display, lush leaves and grasses form a dark foil for vivid red bouvardia flowers, evoking an exotic, jungle-like feel. A square stone pot is lined with ligularia leaves, their glossy surface contrasting with the rough texture of the stone. Place a small glass or plastic container inside the lined pot and fill it with water, then put in the heads of bouvardia, a flower that should never be left out of water. Finally, loop strands of bear grass over the top to look like the handles of a basket, tucking the ends in under the leaves.

Ruby and sapphire

The jewel-like hues of glossy red hypericum berries
and spiky blue sea holly will warm up any room. To give
the colours and textures their full impact, mass flowers
or materials of one type together. Here the sea holly and
berries are arranged in a compact hand-tied bouquet,
with the holly in the centre and the berries forming a
border around it. Take a few stems in your hand, starting
at the centre, then add a few more at a time to build up
the bouquet. Tie with twine, then place in a bowl lined
with a layer of silvery-grey cineraria leaves, which
highlight the colours.

TIP
As an alternative to
hypericum you could use
viburnum berries, which
are a vibrant metallic
shade of blue.

Grass sundae

Dip into the wide selection of grasses now available at florists and you should find plenty of suitable material to make a gorgeous display. Here they spill abundantly from the top of a tall wooden container in an arrangement that resembles a giant ice-cream sundae. The tiny white flowerheads at the base are gypsophila, or baby's breath, while fat furry caterpillars of setaria grass rest just above it. A varied mixture of other grasses, from long and blade-like to soft and feathery, completes the recipe.

TIP
In a predominantly green arrangement of foliage or grasses, including a variety of different textures and shapes is the key to success.

Design detail

Flowers can help to bring a room scheme to life, so choose displays that enhance the interior style you want to create. In this classic bathroom setting, with cream-painted walls and furniture, the blowsy pink peonies and lime-green guelder roses add a welcome splash of colour. Displayed in an old tin jug, which is perched on a wooden stool, they create a decorative feature for a bare corner, with the angular lines of the jug and stool offsetting the curved legs and carved detail of the pretty period-style washstand alongside.

Round it off

Achieving a distinctive shape is one of the hallmarks of successful floral design, especially if you want to create a more formal, traditional-style arrangement. A conical vase makes it easy to set roses in a dome shape, without the need to fiddle around with florist's foam. Strip the leaves and thorns from 18 white roses, then place the outer circle of blooms in place, trimming the stems so that the heads sit against the edge of the vase. Add the next layer, trimming the stems so that the heads are raised just above the first ones. Continue adding layers until the vase is full.

TIP
Most roses available as cut flowers have no fragrance, so if you want scented ones look for the more expensive garden or old-fashioned varieties.

Purple prose

Valued for their delightful fragrance and range of
colours, sweet peas evoke images of old-fashioned
cottage gardens. They look best arranged on their own,
without other foliage or flowers, and here a purple vase
gives a modern edge to a big bunch of scented sweet
peas in the same colour. Be generous with the number of
flowers, and gather them together to form a ball shape
before cutting the stems to length. In this slender vase
the stems are packed in tight, so as to retain the shape.

Global support

Flamboyant white lilies add instant glamour to a room, as well as a rich perfume. They are also tougher than they appear, lasting extremely well as cut flowers. Their long stems give them a stately presence in tall containers, but if you want a more compact arrangement for a smaller room they can be equally effective if cut down, so that the heads rest on the lip of a globe vase. The glossy white surface of this vase works well in contrast with the crazy heads of Casablanca lilies, creating a cool, sophisticated look.

TIP
If you get lily pollen on your clothes, remove it by taking a piece of sticky tape and patting it on the dust. Don't rub, or the pollen will stain.

Big-headed beauties

A low, wide-necked vase such as this goldfish bowl is the best option for flowers with top-heavy heads, such as full-blown peonies. With their stems trimmed short so that their heads are supported by the rim of the vase, blooms in red, pink and white mass together in a glorious explosion of colour. The stems are concealed by a large calathea leaf. First trim the stem of the leaf, then wrap it around your hand and release it inside the vase so that it unfurls close to the glass. Add water, then arrange the peonies, including a few leaves near the neck of the vase.

TIP
If you find it hard to make stems stay in place in a wide-necked vase, make a grid across the top using sticky tape, leaving enough space to insert the stems.

Shaping up

A classic architectural arrangement gets a softer
look with the use of puffball purple alliums and feathery
asparagus fern. The decanter-style vase has a heavy
base, which ensures that the tall display remains stable,
while the narrow neck makes it easy to arrange the
flowers. Trim the stems of five alliums to different
heights, cutting the tallest about three times the height
of the vase and the shortest so that the head rests on
the rim. Add a few fern fronds to soften the outline.

TIP
Allium blooms have a
faint onion odour that
gets stronger as they age.
Take care not to bruise
the flowers when handling
as this will release even
more of the smell.

Slimline

Snow-white peonies with extravagantly layered petals look twice as sumptuous when juxtaposed with the rich purple tint of this glass vase. The ellliptical shape of the vase makes it perfect for narrow window ledges or mantelpieces, and the sturdy base allows it to support heavier displays safely. Cut the peonies so that the lowest heads sit just above the rim and the remaining ones just above these, and include plenty of leaves to provide some background colour for the white flowers.

TIP
If you don't have a tinted vase, try adding a few drops of food dye to the water to get the colour you want.

Vintage chic

A casual country-style gathering of summery garden flowers in glass bottles is given a refined air with the addition of a shiny silver tray. You can pick up vintage glass bottles inexpensively at antiques fairs and flea markets – look for ones with coloured as well as clear glass, and collect a variety of sizes and shapes. Here blue and green bottles echo the colours of the flowers and foliage, which include blue muscari, white sweet peas, dill flower, blue nigella and a selection of grasses.

Perfectly plain

For a look of understated elegance that works well
in both period and contemporary homes, choose plain
containers with gently flowing curves. A white vase that
tapers towards the bottom is perfect for a dome-shaped
arrangement of pastel-coloured roses, punctuated by
a few in a deeper pink. Cut the stems so that the lowest
heads sit just above the rim, with the others resting on
top of them. A few more heads nestling at the base of
a glass jar add to the flower power, while the mirror
throws back reflections of the whole display.

The full works

A tall conical vase has an elegant air in itself, and an exotic arrangement that brings together a tiger-stripe Singapore orchid and calathea leaves more than does it justice. But this display has even more visual excitement to offer, as the base of the vase is filled with iridescent, pearly oyster shells. Decorative pebbles or beads would also look good. This idea means you can get away with using shorter-stemmed, less costly flowers in a tall vase, as the stems are concealed by the shells.

Twice as nice

You can't have too much of a good thing, so try splitting a bouquet of flowers between two identical containers to double its impact. The purple glass of these tall vases makes a perfect foil for cream-coloured anemones, and complements the lilac tones of feathery sea lavender. Fresh green leaves add further colour, and the delicate flowers and foliage are offset by the dark stems, visible through the glass. Group the anemones and leaves at the front of the arrangement, resting their heads on the vase rim, then use the sea lavender at the back to add height.

Light romance

Choose a palette of pale colours to complement a light, airy room. This feminine and fragrant bouquet features white lilac, creamy freesias and pink larkspur, all displayed in an elegant semi-frosted vase. The waisted shape of the vase makes it easy to arrange the flowers. Cut the stems to varying heights to give some shape to the arrangement, but keep the overall look loose. Line up the freesias around the rim of the vase, with the sprays of lilac above them and the tall spires of larkspur fanning out at the back to add height.

Floating world

Some of the best modern arrangements can hardly
be called arrangements at all, as they require so very
little in the way of equipment, or even flowers! Invest
in a shallow glass bowl and you can create numerous
stunning displays simply by filling it half full with water
and floating flowerheads and petals on top. Any blooms
that hold their shape in water are suitable for this idea.
Roses are perfect – in this bowl a large yellow head is
surrounded by a scattering of curling petals in scarlet
and yellow.

Enduring relationship

If you want a display that will last longer than cut
flowers, but are fed up with fussy, dust-gathering dried
flower arrangements, this unusual idea may be more
up your street. For Zen-like simplicity in seconds, fill
a tall cylindrical glass vase about three-quarters full
with monkey nuts, and then stand a single dried cotton
branch among them. You don't even need water. If you
can't find cotton branches, try experimenting with other
natural dried matter, such as interesting seedheads or
sculptural twigs.

Proud line-up

There's power in numbers as they say, so to increase the impact of a super-simple display, all you have to do is repeat it a few times. Slender glass drinking tumblers complement the graceful elegance of pink nerines, whose flowers are a similar shape to lilies but on a much smaller scale. The two nerines in each vase are accompanied by curling stems of bear grass. A line-up of three identical displays makes a chic decoration for a narrow shelf or mantelpiece.

TIP
Nerines are readily available in the winter, so try combining them with traditional Christmas greenery to add an exotic touch to festive decorations.

Dishy number

Team it with a clever choice of containers, and all you need is a single flowerhead to create a stylish display. Think about the combination of colours and textures. In a harmony of muted hues, the iridescent lilac tones of this hydrangea head are offset beautifully by the soft blue of the small bowl in which it sits. At the same time, the delicate quality of its petals is enhanced by contrast with the rough texture of the stone platter. Add a little water to the small bowl to keep the flower fresh.

Poppy art

Flowers with colourful and flamboyant blooms are more than capable of speaking for themselves, so are a brilliant choice if you want an easy display that's guaranteed to brighten up a room in minutes. Papery-petalled Iceland poppies take a bow in a slender glass vase, which is ideal for supporting their tall stems. Simply cut them to different lengths so that each bloom finds its own level. In a display with only a few flowers, make sure that they are all in good condition, with no bruised or torn petals to spoil the effect.

TIP
Poppies can wilt quickly as they lose a lot of sap when cut. To prevent this, seal the ends of the stems by burning them with a match or lighter.

Orient express

The Japanese are masters of simplicity when it comes to flowers and gardens, so take a leaf out of their book for a taste of oriental style. A tall, shapely vase and a few sprigs of fluffy white blossom will put you on the right road in seconds. The tender green twigs are complemented by the dark olive tones of the crackleglaze vase, creating a look that combines a fresh springtime feel with an air of formal elegance. To emphasize the oriental tone, add a bamboo tray and a few pieces of white porcelain.

Sharp looks

Flowers or leaves that boast distinctive shapes, such as this gloriously spiky sea holly, are ideal candidates for simple treatment. A tough character like this doesn't even need an elegant vase to catch the attention. Here a single stem has been slipped into an old glass bottle, which was picked up for just £1 at a market. You may well have similar containers lurking in your kitchen cupboards, such as old sauce bottles or jam jars. Of course, if they've held food, make sure you clean them out properly first.

Bowl 'em over

This one's got it all – it's inexpensive, easy to achieve and simply gorgeous. A few sprays of flowers and greenery is all you need for this beautiful display that highlights the curves of a round glass bowl. Make sure the bowl is sparkling clean, then pour in about 5cm of water. Cut the sprays to size so that they wrap loosely around half the bowl. Place some bear grass in first, then a long strand of variegated ivy, and finally one or two deep blue delphinium spires, tucking all the cut ends into the water.

Cheerful outlook

With their brilliant colours and bold black centres, anemones resemble the sort of flowers that might appear in a child's painting, so are a perfect choice if you want to brighten up a dull corner of a kitchen or family room. An informal display complements their cheery character; simply take a few clear glasses or bottles in varying sizes and slip a few stems into each, resting the flowerheads on the rims of wide-necked tumblers. Group two or three glassfuls together.

TIP
Anemone flowers open in light and heat and close when it is dark and cool. They also incline their heads towards light, so bear these factors in mind when choosing a site for your display.

Bend me, shape me

Capture the carefree mood of spring with a few pretty pink tulips and bendy stems of budding willow, casually intertwined within a glass vase. Pour a small amount of water into the vase, then place three lengths of willow together and curl them around inside. Add three tall tulips, their stems cut to a length of about 60cm, and gently fold each one into an arch shape, making sure you place the stems in the water. As a finishing touch, gently float a few full-blown tulip heads on the surface of the water.

Still waters

Conjure up an air of Zen-like calm with this super-quick display idea for arum lilies. Plain as black and white, yet big on contemporary chic, it uses four white lilies laid horizontally across a square black dish to create an oriental-style arrangement that's as simple as it is stylish. Cut the lily stems to length, then fill the base of a small curved dish with enough water to cover the ends of the stems. Add a handful of shiny black pebbles to hold them in place.

Petal power

This ultra-simple idea takes traditional red roses and uses them in a modern display that would make a perfect focal point for an empty fireplace. All you need to do is strip off the stems and scatter whole heads and petals around a large white candle in the base of a wide glass vase. This is an effective way of using the cheaper small-headed roses, which tend to look rather mean in conventional arrangements. Add to the abundance of red by scattering more petals on the hearth around the base of the vase.

Single-minded

Some people find a whole bunch of sunflowers too bright and garish. If you're among them, try popping a single stem into a sleek bottle vase for a much more subtle option. The base of the glass vase is filled with sand, in a rich terracotta shade that complements the rustic tones of the sunflower. The sand serves to steady the tall vase, while a large test tube embedded within it holds water and supports the long stem of the flower.

Going solo

One exquisite white bloom, one beautiful vase –
bring them together for the perfect fuss-free display.
The visual rewards far outweigh the tiny effort of
filling the vase about a third full with water and floating
a single flowerhead on top. The only 'skill' comes in the
choice of vase and bloom; go for a flower with a large,
showy head, such as this white peony. Any shapely,
wide-necked, clear glass vase will do, but the white
band across the top of this one gives maximum effect
by seeming to enclose and frame the peony while
echoing its colour.

TIP
**The right time to buy
peonies is when the buds
are showing some colour
and feel soft to the touch.
A bud that is too firm will
probably never open.**

Bead necklace

It may seem like cheating, but a single flower in a simple glass vase or tumbler can make as strong a statement as an entire bouquet. If you want to show your friends that a little more creative thought has gone into the display, add a decorative touch by floating some brightly coloured beads on the surface of the water. Here the red beads are an exact match for the colour of the raggedy-topped carnation, creating an effect that's effortlessly elegant.

TIP
Cut carnation stems between the nodes, the thick, fibrous parts where buds or leaves emerge. This allows water to penetrate the stem more easily.

Trendsetters

One way to ensure that your flower displays are bang up to date is to look for cutting-edge containers. There are new breeds of vases out there that make it simple to create designer-style looks. The curvaceous model at the back is almost entirely enclosed, with one opening at each end, while the vase in the foreground is a ball of glass punctuated with two openings. Invest in containers like these, then save money on flowers – all they need is a few distinctive blooms such as these claret-coloured dahlias. Stems of zig-zag asparagus fern add a softer touch.

TIP
Flowers of one type in a vase will last longer than a mix of different varieties, and a single bloom will survive longer than many heads of the same kind.

Glass act

The beauty of a hand-tied bouquet is that it can be put straight into a vase for a simply stunning display. Encasing the entire thing in a tall tank gives a cool, contemporary twist to this cheery bunch of yellow tulips. Take about 20 stems and arrange them so that the heads are at different levels. Trim all the stems to the same length and tie the bouquet with raffia. To make a glass showcase, find a tank vase tall and wide enough to take the full height of the tulips and fill it with water to just below the first flowerheads.

TIP
Always re-cut the stems of a bouquet you have been given before arranging the flowers in water. This opens up fresh fibres that take up the water more easily.

Summer nights

When the weather warms up and dining moves outdoors, treat your guests to a candlelit feast accompanied by a few of these enchanting table decorations. Summer flowers and twinkling tealights are sure to bring out the romance of balmy evenings and, best of all, they can be assembled in minutes. Place a simple glass tumbler on a saucer and pour a small amount of water into both. Pick the heads off a selection of summer flowers, and arrange them with a few leaves in the saucer. Float a tealight on the water in the glass.

Winter wonderland

Take a break from traditional reds and golds at Christmas and go for a cooler look with white roses, spiky purple sea holly, silver-painted twigs and a few sculptural seedheads. Bring it all together in a loose arrangement, adding plenty of dark green leaves and a few sprays of variegated ivy, then display in a plain white vase. The simple detailing around the top of this tall container adds a suggestion of snowflakes. For extra glitz, pile a few silver and purple baubles in a white bowl and place it alongside the arrangement.

TIP
Paint dried material such as twigs and pine cones using spray paints. Work in a well-ventilated room and cover surrounding surfaces well.

Christmas classic

Make this formal candle centrepiece as a focal point for your Christmas table. Take a shallow circular glass dish and cut pre-soaked florist's foam to fit, making it a little narrower than the bowl's diameter, but 1cm taller. Tuck wide tropical green leaves down the sides, then add more water. Insert three candles centrally in the foam, using special candleholders available from florists. Add pine, holly and poppy seedheads, letting them trail over the edge. Group roses loosely into threes, cut the stems to 15cm and place among the greenery. Tie ribbon bows onto wire and insert at intervals.

To complement the centrepiece, make ties for plain white napkins using a red rose attached with wire to a twist of ivy.

Stalk talk

The stems make almost as much impact as the flowers when a clear glass vase is used to display this colourful hand-held bouquet. Prepare red, orange and pink roses by removing the thorns and leaves. Lay the first stem in the palm of your hand and add more roses, turning the bunch as you go. Finally, add large waxy leaves so that they lie beneath the flowers. Secure the bouquet with twine or an elastic band, trim the stems level and place in a vase with a narrow neck, splaying out the stems from the base.

Best of the bunch

Hand-tied bouquets are an easy way of creating elegant arrangements, whether to decorate your own home or to wrap up and give as a gift. The most pleasing examples feature flowers and foliage in a range of textures and sizes, and this colourful bunch includes pink roses, cockscomb, flowering mint and dill. Lay the main blooms across the palm of your left hand, then set more flowers at a slight diagonal. Continue to build up the bouquet, rotating it in your hand until it is the size you want. Tie firmly with twine, then trim the stems to a similar length.

Instant sparkle

If you haven't time to make an elaborate decoration
for your Christmas table, glam it up in minutes with
a handful of flowerheads and some twinkling sequins.
Half fill a shallow glass bowl with water, then cover the
base with glass beads and float a layer of sequins on
top. Snip off a few impressive flowerheads such as roses
and lilies and float these in the water. Secure a few more
sequins to the petals with drops of water, then surround
the dish with tealights in small pearlized bowls.

Festive welcome

Dress your front door for Christmas with a wreath
that combines traditional berried ivy and snowberries
with more unusual blue thistles and lilac freesias.
Soak an Oasis wreath frame in water, then cut 15cm
stems of berried ivy and snowberries and fix them
into the foam until it is completely covered. Intersperse
with thistles and freesias, adding more until the wreath
looks full and balanced. Add a touch of sparkle with
embroidery stones, available from craft shops, by gluing
them onto the ivy leaves using a small amount of clear
all-purpose adhesive.

**Oasis wreath frames
are cheaply available
from florists and garden
centres. Follow the
manufacturer's soaking
instructions before
inserting the flowers
and foliage.**

Snow white

Paper whites are widely available at Christmas, and
this flower and candle combination makes a fresh,
modern alternative to traditional festive displays.
Place a large pillar candle in a flat-based glass bowl.
Make four bunches of paper whites by gathering a few
stems in your hand, then adding more to form a ball
of flowerheads. Tie with string, and cut the stems so
the flowers sit on the rim of the bowl. Wrap aspidistra,
yucca or laurel leaves around the stems of each bunch
and bind with golden wire. Place the 'flower trees'
around the candle and fill the bowl with water.

Feminine touch

This pretty bouquet, full of enchanting pastel colours and spring fragrance, would make a delightful Mother's Day present. Group together parrot tulips, hyacinths and folded aspidistra leaves into a posy, starting from the centre by holding a few blooms in your hand, then alternating the flowers and foliage as you build up the bouquet. Cut the stems to similar lengths and tie with string. Finish by wrapping gossamer-fine tissue paper around the flowers – you'll need about three sheets – and secure with a pink or lilac ribbon tied into a bow.

TIP
Hyacinth stems secrete a poisonous latex, so wear gloves when handling them or wash your hands immediately afterwards.

Rosy posy

With their luxuriously multi-petalled heads, rich colours and romantic associations, roses are the perfect choice for a really special gift bouquet. If you want to treat someone, take about 20 roses, remove any thorns and leaves, and mass them together into a posy, twisting the stems and tying them in the middle with a narrow ribbon. To add a bit of decoration, take a roll of fine silver wire and make twisted knots at 10cm intervals. Wrap the wire gently around the head of the posy and secure the ends among the stems.

TIP
Removing rose thorns is necessary if you're making a bouquet but it can damage the stems, so ease them off very carefully using a sharp knife.

Heavenly scent

Put together this aromatic posy as a gift – or make it for yourself and display in a galvanized planter, which forms a steely contrast for the pastel flowerheads. Take about 10 pink and white garden roses, plus variegated ivy and fragrant foliage such as eucalyptus and rosemary. Starting with a few flowers at the centre, work outwards, building up the posy in your hand to form a rounded shape. Secure the stems with string, then trim them all to the same length. Display in the planter so that the posy rests on the rim, with the outer blooms hiding its edge.

Funtime

Formal bouquets are fine for special occasions, but if you simply want to cheer someone up you can't beat a casual collection of cottage-garden favourites. Have fun with bold hues, choosing a zappy colour combination such as sky-blue delphiniums and orange snapdragons. Bring them together to make an informal bouquet, by taking a few stems in your hand and adding a few more at a time, finally encircling the flowers with hosta leaves at the base. Tie with brightly coloured twine and trim all the stems to the same length.

TIP
If you want to make a smaller arrangement, you could swap the delphiniums for blue cornflowers or lilac Chinese asters.

In the can

Get into the habit of saving old food cans and you'll have a constant supply of quirky containers just waiting for the right flowers to come along. Where would you find a more appropriate holder for an exuberant bunch of summer sunflowers than an old sunflower oil can? This one has an illustration to provide a double helping of blooms and a green background that's a perfect match for the leaves. Use a tin opener to remove the top if necessary, then clean the can thoroughly before filling with water. Look out for sharp edges left by the tin opener when handling.

Squash game

Filled with fiery Chinese lanterns to light up a room, a hollowed-out butternut squash makes an original natural container. Slice a sliver off the bottom of the squash to create a flat base and make it stand, then cut off the top and scoop out enough of the vegetable matter to hold and hide a small vase. Put some water in the vase and slot the lanterns in place. Any other large fruits or vegetables that have firm skins could also lead a double life as vases – try watermelons or pumpkins, for example.

TIP
If your vegetable vase seems a little wobbly, stick a few pieces of Blu-Tack to the base to help it stand firm.

Bright beakers

A search through your kitchen cupboards can often turn up some cool containers. Floral flair relies on dash rather than cash, and a successful marriage of flowers and vases is more important than the elegance of one or the other. Even humble plastic beakers can shine when teamed up with the right flowers. These ones in brilliant green and blue complement perfectly the hot pinks and purples of anemones. Cut the flower stems so that the heads rest on the rim of the beaker. Place a few of these colourful arrangements side by side to brighten up a shelf or windowsill.

Net results

There's no need to limit your search for original containers to those that can hold water. This mesh bag looks the business, while the purple hyacinths and anemones get their drink from a pint glass hidden inside. To make the bouquet, take six hyacinths and 18 anemones. Hold a couple of stems in your hand, then add more so that they form a spiral. When the bouquet is complete, secure the stems with an elastic band, then trim them all to the same length. Place the flowers inside the glass, fill it with water, and slip the glass into the bag.

Rescue mission

A windy day in a cottage garden can leave odd blooms broken off. Don't let them go to waste – pick them quickly and arrange in an assortment of glass bottles in different sizes and shapes, the more traditional the better. Here pink veronica, deep red snapdragon, white allium, dusty pink helleborus and a purple sweet pea all go into the mix, and are shown off in jam jars and old drinks bottles made from clear and green glass. If you can't find suitable glassware at home, see what you can pick up at markets or car boot sales.

Metal magic

If you have trouble arranging flowers in wide-necked vases, these easy-to-make metal covers could help. Create a template by drawing around the rim of your vase on paper, then draw out from this to design the sides of the cover. Cut out the template and use it to cut the same shape from thin metal. Mark around the edges with a pen, then cut out the design with small sharp scissors. Using a six-ways punch, make evenly spaced holes for flowers in the top part of the cover and decorate the side edges with tiny holes. Place over the vase and fold down the edges.

Get the wrap

If you're bored with your old vases or they look too fussy for contemporary floral designs, give them an instant update with a wrapping of fresh white fabric. Take any upright vase and loosely swathe it with a fine white material such as muslin or voile. Be generous with the amount of fabric to create a flamboyant look and thoroughly conceal the vase. Secure by binding it with wire or cord. Choose matching white flowers for a sophisticated display – here tulips and ranunculus are teamed with lysimachia and silver-painted ting ting.

TIP
For a more sumptuous look, wrap your vase in richly coloured silk. Fill it with bold blooms such as roses or peonies in strong coordinating shades.

Take the tube

Test tubes are just the right size and shape to hold
a single flower stem, and are also cheap to buy. Get a
collection of them and use lengths of ribbon or raffia
to suspend them from a shelf, curtain rail or window
frame. Tie the ribbon or raffia securely around each
tube and attach it to the underside of a shelf or
frame with drawing pins. Use a jug to partially fill
the tubes with water, then slip in the blooms. Flowers
with fine stems, such as roses, sweet peas or freesias,
are the most suitable.

TIP
**You could use this idea to
decorate your Christmas
tree. Hang the tubes from
the branches using gold or
silver wire or glitzy parcel
ties instead of raffia.**

Triple treat

Team shiny tin cans with stately delphinium spires and line them up on a mantelpiece or along a dinner table to make a dramatic modern display. Save three identical food cans, then clean them out and soak off the labels. Cut blocks of florist's foam to fit in the cans, leaving space at the top for pebbles, then soak the foam in water before placing inside. Cut three delphinium stems the same length and insert into the foam. Conceal the foam with a layer of white pebbles.

TIP
If possible, choose cans with ring-pull lids – these won't have the sharp, jagged edge left by a tin opener.

Pretty in pink

Matching your vases to the colour of the flowers creates a powerful impression, and dressing them up in fabric makes it easy to achieve that coordinated look. Stiff gauze wrapped around clear glass tubes echoes the delicate pink of these tulip heads. Sheer enough to diffuse the light, it also allows a glimpse of the long graceful stems. Cut a piece of fabric large enough to wrap around the vase, allowing for a small overlap, then secure neatly with clear glue. For maximum impact, group a few tubes together, with a single tulip stem, complete with leaf, in each.

TIP
Tulips will bend their
heads towards the light
so turn the vase daily
to keep them straight.

Tangerine dream

The graduated orange effect on these glass vases may look as though it has come straight out of a designer's studio, but anyone can achieve it using a can of spray paint. Work in a well-ventilated area and cover surrounding surfaces with newspaper. It's a good idea to spray the vase inside a large open cardboard box to avoid too much mess. Choose a vase with a smooth surface and apply light coats until you are satisfied with the effect. For a graduated look, direct the spray at the point where you want the densest colour – around the rim or base.

Bags of tricks

Glassware or china departments are the obvious places to search for containers, but look elsewhere and you may come home with some interesting finds. Have you tried your local candle store, for example? There are lots of pretty paper and fabric votive candleholders around, which make great little vases. These mesh bags have a glass inside intended to hold the candle, but it's also just the right size to accommodate a single flower with a big bright head, such as a carnation. Repetition increases the impact so place a row of at least six down the centre of a dining table or along a mantelpiece.

Putting on the glitz

Pop one or two flamboyant flowerheads into a sequined handbag to make a sparkling display that would be perfect for glamming up a bedroom. Hydrangeas have the panache to carry off this quirky idea, and with the delicate lilac petals picking up on the colour of the bag, flowers and container look as if they were made for one another. To hold and nourish the blooms, place a drinking glass or empty jam jar inside the bag and add water, or make a waterproof lining using a plastic bag and fill it with pre-soaked florist's foam.

Veggie showstopper

Ornamental cabbages have the looks to lift them out of
the vegetable patch and into a starring role as pot plants.
With a collar of frilly leaves cradling a bright pink centre,
they are sure to capture the attention, and will add a
touch of drama to any room. For a hint of potting-shed
ruggedness, wrap their pots in plastic and then cover
this with jute scrim. Wrap a length of it around the pots
a few times, then tie with raffia. Jute scrim is available
from builders' merchants.

Feeling hot

Bring a dash of spice into your home with red-hot chilli peppers and solanum, whose berries resemble small tomatoes. Plant them in square or round galvanized metal tins for a back-to-roots Mexican flavour. Grown for their decorative fruits, capsicums, or ornamental peppers, are usually sold at Christmas, although summer-flowering types are also available. The fruits darken with age from yellow to orange before they finally turn red. Solanum plants are also popular during the festive season, and their round berries turn from green to orange-red.

Leaf dressing

When the winter chill is still in full swing outside,
it's lovely to see potted bulbs shooting up indoors
and opening their buds to proclaim the start of spring.
Daffodils and narcissus can be planted indoors or out,
although they last longer outside. Plant the bulbs in
autumn, to flower the following spring. If your regular
houseplants have laid claim to all your stylish pots, pick
up a few large waxy leaves from your local florist and
use these to conceal unattractive plastic containers.
Fix one end to the pot with sticky tape, then wrap the
leaf around and tie with raffia.

TIP
**If you find it difficult
to keep the leaf in
place, fix it to the pot
more securely using a
little double-sided
sticky tape.**

Goldfish bowl garden

Make a decorative planter for succulents using a goldfish bowl. Put a line of masking tape around the inside, about a third of the way up, and paint the inside surface of the bowl green below this line using household satinwood paint. Continue the paint over the lower edge of the tape to ensure that you get a clean line. When the paint is dry, remove the masking tape and fill the bowl up to this line with plant compost. Plant an aloe vera flanked by a couple of small cacti, then scatter coloured mosaic or broken tiles over the surface of the compost.

Clear winners

Sculptural plants such as succulents suit modern interiors well, so give them trendy containers to match. Browse around the homeware stores, and you'll find it easy to pick up some original ideas; these clear acrylic containers are intended for storing stationery, yet they do a perfect job as planters. Fill them with white gravel, then bury the roots and soil of the succulents among the gravel so that they're not visible. Cacti and succulents should be watered frequently between spring and autumn but only sparingly in winter.

TIP
Rather than burying the roots and soil in the gravel, you may find it easier to leave the plants in their original pots and simply conceal these among the stones.

Go-anywhere plant

With their beautiful flowers on tall stems, potted lilies are extremely versatile. They look elegant in understated classic interiors or minimalist modern rooms, but are also striking enough to hold their own among brilliant colours and modern decor. This fragrant pot variety, *Lilium oriental*, has flowers splashed with pink that echoes the vibrant shade on the wall behind, while its lime-green pot provides a zingy contrast. Lily pollen can stain clothes and carpets, so you may want to remove the stamens – do this by pulling them off with your fingers. Water the plant moderately and feed lightly once a week.

TIP
When they have finished flowering, pot lilies can be planted out in the garden in a semi-shaded spot. They will flower again the following year.

Seventies revival

Firm favourites in 1970s homes, spider plants later fell out of fashion, but now these easy-to-grow plants are being appreciated for their retro appeal. Give them an instant update by displaying them in brightly coloured rattan pots. Place in a light, sunny spot, then keep them supplied with lots of water and a weekly feed, and they will reward you with the familiar cascade of fine leaves. In addition, the flowering stems produce miniature plants, which can easily be removed and propagated to make new ones. The club-like roots should be repotted every year.

TIP
Spider plants can rid an enclosed space of carbon monoxide, so use them to combat traffic fumes by lining up a few pots along a windowsill.

Flame effect

Add a flicker of warmth to a pale neutral colour scheme with the brilliant flame-like flowers of this showy bromeliad. Vrieseas are native to Central and South America, so this stripy, ethnic-inspired pot makes a fitting container, reflecting the plant's origins and balancing the bright colours of its leaves and flowers. In the wild, vrieseas are adaptable plants, thriving in both damp forests and cooler, dry regions, but indoors they do best in a warm, humid atmosphere. The roots should be kept moist but not wet; if possible, use water that has been boiled and then allowed to cool to a lukewarm temperature.

Stripe tease

Follow through the trend for stripes in the home with a neoregelia plant. Some varieties, like this one, have variegated stripes running the length of their leaves. Another striking asset is the pink or red colour of the rosette of leaves at the centre, which also has tiny flowers hidden inside. These bromeliads come from the Amazon region and like temperatures of around 20°C and a bright position, although not direct sunlight. Water moderately into the rosette as well as the compost, feed once a month and mist the leaves regularly with a spray bottle.

Blending in

Delicate plants with classic looks, such as this pretty
pot rose, can be made to look perfectly at home in
a punchy modern setting if displayed in the right
containers. Try simple transparent holders made from
clear glass or plastic, concealing the roots and compost
among a soft bed of spongy moss. Pot roses flower well
in a light spot, as long as they are kept moist and fed
once a week. To encourage regrowth, cut the plant back
to 5cm above the soil after it has finished flowering, and
two months later you should see new flowers.

Shine on

An attractive plant can be a welcome addition to a home office, adding a natural touch among all the sleek machinery and other equipment. The smooth, mirror-like surface of a shiny metallic pot heightens that textural contrast, offsetting the ribbed leaves and spiky orange flowers of this *Calathea crocata*. One of the few calatheas that produce flowers, its leaves have bronze-maroon undersides and close up at night. Place it in a light position but not full sun, in a temperature of around 20°C. Spray regularly and water sparingly.

TIP
Using hard water will cause water marks to appear on the leaves of calathea plants, so give them boiled water that has been allowed to cool.

Peace offering

Tall and serene, with shapely white flowers and long shiny leaves, the peace lily will make its presence felt in any room, and is more than capable of standing out against a brightly painted backdrop. To make the most of its height, plant it in a tall pot; the slick style and sharp colour of this planter is ideal for a bold, modern setting. Peace lilies need a lot of water and should also be sprayed occasionally, avoiding the flowers. Feed them once a fortnight. If you remove dead flowers regularly, new ones should appear after four to six weeks.

TIP
Many plants suffer from dry air in centrally heated rooms, so misting the leaves, if recommended, is an important care routine. Placing pots in groups also helps to increase humidity levels.

PRACTICAL ADVICE

Steps to success

Today's trends in floral design play right into the hands of those of us too busy to fuss over formal arrangements. Simple and natural are the keywords, and as the displays in this book prove, you don't have to spend hours juggling shape, form and colour to produce spectacular looks. However, a few minutes devoted to preparing flowers and containers will keep your handiwork fresh and healthy for as long as possible. Seeing that flowers never go thirsty and giving some thought to where you place your display will also extend its life. The following tips will help you give cut flowers the care they appreciate, so that they reward you with long-lasting looks. Individual varieties may have additional care requirements, so ask your florist for advice if you want to get the best from your blooms.

Buying fresh flowers

• To be sure of getting good-quality, long-lasting flowers, buy them from a reputable professional florist.

• Look for firm petals and healthy green leaves. Most flowers should be bought when they are in bud or half open, and buds should show a reasonable amount of colour. Ones that are too tight may never open.

• Bouquets should be well wrapped to protect the flowers. If it will be several hours before you can put them in water, ask the florist to cover the ends of the stems with damp paper. Flowers can also be 'aqua packed', with a pod of water around the stems.

• Check that cut flower food is included with your blooms, and ask for some if not. It usually comes in powder form, in a small plastic sachet but is also available as a liquid.

Conditioning bought blooms

• Don't rush to arrange your flowers as soon as you get them home. A little time spent preparing them, known as conditioning, will help to extend their lifespan.

• Remove all the lower leaves and cut each stem at an angle a couple of centimetres from its end. As soon as you have done this, place them in a bucket of deep, tepid water for six to eight hours to give them a good drink. (NB Generally cut flowers prefer tepid water with the exception of spring flowers. These should be always treated with cold water.)

• If stems are bent, you can straighten them by tightly wrapping the whole bunch in brown paper and securing it with sticky tape before placing the flowers in the water.

Flowers from your garden

• The best time to pick flowers is in the early morning or late evening, when the sun is low, the air is cool and the stems hold more water. Flowers cut in the heat of the day may wilt more quickly.

• Use secateurs or sharp scissors, and cut thicker stems or thin branches at an angle.

• Place the flowers and foliage in water immediately after cutting, otherwise air-locks can form in the stems, reducing their ability to take in water. If necessary, carry a bucket outdoors with you, filled with tepid water that comes up to the flowers' necks. Leave them in the bucket for up to 12 hours before arranging.

Preparing containers

• Make sure that vases are thoroughly cleaned before each use as any lingering bacteria will harm fresh flowers.

• If you are using an unusual container, check that it is watertight. If not, line it with a jar or tumbler. (Some metals, such as zinc, can be toxic to flowers so it's best to line all metal containers just in case.)

• Choose a container that will be able to hold sufficient water to feed the number of flowers you are using.

• Fill your chosen container with lukewarm water, unless you are arranging spring bulb flowers such as daffodils or tulips, which prefer it cold.

• Sprinkle in the cut flower food supplied by the florist, which is designed to nourish the flowers, help them last and prevent bacteria build-up. Use the correct amount for your size of container. Don't be tempted to try suggestions for home-made flower foods as these do more harm than good.

Arranging flowers

• To keep the water in the vase clean, make sure any leaves below water level have been stripped off, as rotting greenery will encourage harmful bacteria.

• When you cut stems to length, snip diagonally to give them a larger surface area for absorbing water.

• Florist's foam, such as Oasis, is useful if you are creating a more formal arrangement with a distinctive shape, and want to ensure that each flower keeps its position. It comes in blocks that can be cut to fit your container, and the dense foam is able to absorb a significant amount of water to keep the flowers fresh. Soak it before arranging them, following the manufacturer's instructions.

• Another, simpler way of keeping flowers in place is to put scrunched-up chicken wire inside the vase.

Perfect positioning

• Flowers are used to being outdoors, so keep your display in a cool place, away from direct sunlight and hot radiators. Tight buds need sufficient light to open, but once they have done so, move them to a less bright position.

• Keep your flowers away from bowls of fruit. Ripening fruit emits a small amount of ethylene gas which causes cut flowers to age prematurely. Dying flowers have the same effect on fresh displays.

• Never place a vase of flowers directly on top of electrical equipment or polished furniture in case of unexpected leaks.

Looks that last

• To ensure that your flowers last as long as possible, top up the water (with food added) whenever necessary. Some flowers will make the water murky within a few days. If this happens empty and rinse out the vase and refill it.

• Pinch off dead flowers and leaves to encourage other blooms to open and to prolong the life of your arrangement.

• Vase life varies for different flowers so ask your florist's advice if you want to create a display that will be at its peak for a special occasion.

STOCKISTS:

FLORISTRY SUNDRIES AND CRAFT SUPPLIES

BUTTERCUPS AND DAISIES
Wide range of floristry sundries including floral foam, bouquet holders, basketry, craft supplies and tools.
Tel: 01202 672200
www.buttercups-daisies.co.uk

BUYRITE
Suppliers of flower pots, raffia, ribbon and florist's foam.
Tel: 01932 349515
www.buyrite.co.uk

CREATIVE BEADCRAFT
Specialist company offering a wide range of beads, sequins and trimmings available by mail order.
Tel: 01494 778818
www.creativebeadcraft.co.uk

FLOWER EXPERTS
Stockists of florist's foam, ribbon, candles and other sundries, cut flowers and bouquets by mail order.
Tel: 0845 140 0001
www.flowerexperts.com

FLOWERS FOREVER
Specialists in 3D flower preservation. Special occasion flowers – such as a bridal bouquets – can be preserved as keepsakes.
Tel: 0800 298 5880
www.flowersforever.co.uk

FLORAL PRODUCTS
Floristry sundries, ribbon, silk flowers, candles, containers and coloured gravel.
www.floral-products.com

GLOBAL FLOWERS
Floral sundries, artificial flowers and foliage.
Tel: 01543 423303
www.globalflowers.co.uk

HAWKIN & CO
Suppliers of candle sand, for ornamental use.
Tel: 01986 782536

HOMECRAFTS DIRECT
Wide range of craft products available by mail order.
Tel: 0116 269 7733
www.homecrafts.co.uk

JET SUPPLIES
Florist's foam, ribbon, baskets, flower food, twines and wire.
Tel: 01275 474516
www.jetsupplies.demon.co.uk

LONDON GRAPHIC CENTRE
Specialist shop offering a range of art and craft sundries and a selection of handmade papers.
Tel: 020 7759 4500
www.londongraphics.co.uk

THE MOSAIC WORKSHOP
Suppliers of mosaic tiles.
Tel: 020 7272 2446
www.mosaicworkshop.com

OSTRICHES ONLINE
Natural and dyed feathers by mail order.
www.ostriches.online.co.uk

PAPERCHASE
Modern and design-conscious stationery retailers offering a good range of tissue papers, ribbons, twines and containers.
Tel: 020 7467 6200 for branches or 0161 839 1500 for mail order
www.paperchase.co.uk

PLASTI-KOTE SPRAY PAINTS
Makers of aerosol spray paints for decorative use, including sprays suitable for use on glass vases and containers.
Tel: 01223 836400
www.spraypaint.co.uk

PRICE'S CANDLES
Wide range of decorative, scented, traditional and garden candles.
Tel: 01234 264500
www.prices-candles.co.uk

FLORISTRY SUNDRIES AND CRAFT SUPPLIES

SMITCRAFT
Suppliers of floristry
accessories, including foam,
ribbons and raffias.
Tel: 01252 342626
www.smitcraft.com

SPECIALIST CRAFTS
Stockists of a wide range of
craft products.
Tel: 0116 269 7711 for stockists,
0161 269 7733 for mail order
www.speccrafts.co.uk

VV ROULEAUX
Wide selection of ribbons,
braids, raffias, feathers, sequins
and trims.
Tel: 020 76274455
www.vvrouleaux.com

WAX LYRICAL
Decorative candles and
candleholders.
Tel: 020 8561 0235

VASES AND CONTAINERS

Bhs
Range of inexpensive vases, dishes and containers in a variety of materials .
Tel: 020 7262 3288
www.bhs.co.uk

BOMBAY DUCK
Makers of unusual beaded boxes and baskets, candle votives and aluminium stem vases.
Tel: 020 8749 8001
www.bombayduck.co.uk

THE CONRAN SHOP
Stockists of contemporary vases, bowls and containers.
Tel: 020 7589 7401
www.conran.co.uk

THE COTSWOLD COMPANY
Mail order company offering a range of baskets and other storage accessories suitable for use as plant containers.
Tel: 01252 391 404
www.cotswoldco.com

DARTINGTON CRYSTAL
Glass vases and hand-crafted glass bowls for smaller arrangements.
Tel: 01805 626262
www.dartington.co.uk

DEBENHAMS
Contemporary homewares including vases, dishes, bowls and candles.
Tel: 020 7408 4444
www.debenhams.com

HABITAT
A good selection of contemporary vases and planters.
Tel: 0845 601 0740
www.habitat.co.uk

HEAL'S
Modern range of designer vases and containers.
Tel: 020 7636 1666
www.heals.co.uk

IKEA
Budget vases and plastic containers.
Tel: 020 8208 5600
www.ikea.co.uk

VASES AND CONTAINERS

JOHN LEWIS
Wide range of vases, containers and woven baskets.
Tel: 020 7629 7711
www.johnlewis.co.uk

LSA INTERNATIONAL
Contemporary glass and porcelain vases.
Tel: 01932 789721
www.lsa-international.com

MARKS & SPENCER
Wide range of contemporary and classic home accessories, including vases, bowls and other containers.
Tel: 020 7935 4422 for stockists or 0845 603 1603 for mail order
www.marksandspencer.com

MONSOON HOME
Vases, bowls and boxes with an ethnic feel.
Tel: 020 7313 3000
www.monsoon.co.uk

MUJI
Japanese-style bowls and dishes, acrylic containers.
Tel: 020 7221 9360
www.muji.co.uk

NEST
A selection of stylish, contemporary vases
Tel: 01392 204305
www.nestinteriors.com

NEXT HOME
Contemporary home accessories including vases and bowls.
Tel: 0870 243 5435 for stockists, 0845 600 7000 for mail order
www.next.co.uk

SOPHIE HANNA FLOWERS
Wide range of unusual vases and other glassware available for bulk purchase or hire.
Tel: 020 7720 0841
www.sophiehannaflowers.com

THE PIER
Range of metal, ceramic and wood vases and containers with a global influence.
Tel: 0845 609 1234
www.pier.co.uk

DEBENHAMS

On-line flower delivery service offering a wide selection of traditional and contemporary bouquets and arrangements plus a designer range.
Tel: 020 7408 4444
www.debenhams.com

FLOWERGRAM

International floral delivery network.
Tel:. 01384 446 342
www.flowergram.co.uk

FLOWER EXPERTS

Cut flowers and bouquets by mail order.
Tel: 0845 140 0001
www.flowerexperts.com

INTERFLORA

One of the world's largest and most popular flower delivery networks.
Tel: 0115 903 5665
www.interflora.co.uk

MARKS & SPENCER

On-line and telephone flower delivery service offering a wide selection of traditional and contemporary fresh flowers, including hand-tied bouquets, flower and planted baskets.
Tel: 0845 603 1603
www.marksandspencer.com

NEXT DIRECTORY

Contemporary selection of fresh flower bouquets delivered direct to your door.
Tcl: 0845 600 7000
www.next.co.uk

WEB FLORISTS

On-line directory of over 8,000 UK florists who will deliver.
Tel: 01342 313222
www.webflorists.co.uk

FLORAL DELIVERY

FLORISTS WHO INSPIRE

BLUEBIRD FLOWER MARKET
Superb fragrant flower market in the King's Road, London.
Tel: 020 7559 1141
www.conran.com

GREEN
Inspirational, contemporary floristry.
Tel: 020 7603 0414

HEAVENLY SCENT FLORAL DESIGNS
Specialists in flowers for weddings, events and conference.
Tel: 01730 892161
www.heavenly-scent.co.uk

JAMES JAMES-CROOK
An inspired 'floral architect'.
Tel: 01903 883239
www.pineappleheads.com

JANE PACKER
One of the world's leading and best-known florists.
Tel: 020 7935 2673
www.jane-packer.co.uk

MARCUS CRANE FLOWERS
Tel: 07973 296860
www.marcuscraneflowers.com

MCQUEENS
Modern, trend-setting florist.
Tel: 020 7252 5500
www.mcqueens.co.uk

PAULA PRYKE FLOWERS
Innovative floral designs and arrangements.
Tel: 020 7837 7336
www.paula-pryke-flowers.com

SOPHIE HANNA FLOWERS
London-based florist specializing in conferences, events, parties and weddings.
Tel: 020 7720 0841
www.sophiehannaflowers.com

ROCKETT
Innovative contemporary floral designs and arrangements.
Tel: 0208 671 9091

FLORISTRY SCHOOLS

JANE PACKER FLOWER SCHOOL

Leading florist Jane Packer's london-based floristry school offers a wide range of courses to suit beginners and experienced florists alike. Programme includes everything from 1-day courses to 4-week career courses.
Tel: 020 7486 1300
www.jane-packer.co.uk

MCQUEENS FLOWER SCHOOL

Contemporary floristry school offering a very varied and challenging series of floristry courses for both beginners and experienced florists.
Tel: 020 8510 0123
www.mcqueens.co.uk

PAULA PRYKE FLOWER SCHOOL

Well-known florist Paul Pryke's London-based floristry school offers a wide range of courses from morning workshops to the prestigious 20-day career course.
Tel: 020 7837 7373
www.paula-pryke-flowers.com

ADVICE AND INFORMATION

THE NATIONAL ASSOCIATION OF FLOWER ARRANGEMENT SOCIETIES (NAFAS)

Organization that provides details of flower shows, flower arranging clubs, subscriptions to specialist floristry magazines and offers an on-line shop on its website.
Tel: 020 7247 5567
www.nafas.org.uk

FLOWERS & PLANTS ASSOCIATION

The UK's promotional organization for cut flowers and indoor plants. Contact them for inspirational ideas, care tips and seasonal trends.
Tel: 020 7738 8044
www.flowers.org.uk

CONTRIBUTORS

BBC Worldwide and *BBC Good Homes* magazine would like to thank the following contributors.

Marcus Crane Flowers: pages 33, 35, 89, 93, 133 Green: pages 103, 105, 135, 161, 163, 187, 189 Jane Hughes (at Rockett): pages 9, 11, 13, 15, 17, 47, 49, 55, 79, 81, 83, 107, 109, 111, 113, 115, 117, 145 165, 167, 169,173

Jane Packer: pages 19, 21, 23, 25, 27, 29, 31, 61, 63, 87, 121, 123, 127, 129, 131, 151, 153, 155, 179, 183, 185 Kate Kenyan (Plants &Flowers Association): pages 37, 39, 41,43, 45, 67, 69, 71, 73, 75, 77, 99, 101, 159, 197, 199, 201, 203, 205, 207, 209

KINGS & PRESIDENTS

POLITICS AND THE KINGDOM OF GOD

TIMOTHY R. GAINES &
SHAWNA SONGER GAINES

Please accept this gift as our way of saying thanks for being a small group email subscriber!

[9780563522591/18]